# Righteousness, the Pathway to Paradise

Richard DeGiacomo

D1715164

Editing and typesetting: Sally Hanan of Inksnatcher.com
Cover design: German Creative

Righteousness, the Pathway to Paradise/Richard DeGiacomo

ISBN  9798441600583

*To Elaine, for all your help and encouragement*

# Table of Contents

# Preface

What is the meaning and purpose of life? What a complex question that is—one that philosophers and researchers have struggled with for thousands of years. Because of my Christian faith, the undisputable answer for me is that life is a gift from God—an omnipotent and benevolent power to be forever embraced and worshiped.

Our existence can be considered an inheritance that is overflowing with divine love, grace, and guidance. It is having a purpose of achievement through righteousness, with closure being eternity in paradise. It is important to know that the objectives we seek will be a major factor in determining our final and everlasting destination.

What could be more meaningful and reassuring than knowing that life is not over when we take our last breath? Many times, I have been asked a question that can be considered among the most important anyone could have: What happens when we die? *The answer can only be that it depends on what happens* before *we die.*

Is that a question you might have? If so, you certainly are not alone. It is my opinion that most people believe in heaven and salvation through Jesus, but because of our humanity, they have a natural, ever-present anxiety of what has been revealed but not experienced. I pray that by the time you have finished reading this book, that anxiety will be eliminated or minimized through the total acceptance of God's Word.

*Richard*

# 1

# What Happens When We Die?

*It is appointed for men to die once, but after this the judgment.*
—Hebrews 9:27

No, life will not be over; death is just the beginning of an everlasting, eternal existence of either salvation or damnation. Of course, we all would want the former, but unfortunately, that will not always be the result, for the way to salvation is through Jesus Christ. Jesus, throughout His ministry, told His apostles that to fulfill what had been prophesied, He must die and after three days be bodily raised. Forty days later, He would be assumed into heaven. By doing so, He conquered death. He also gave us forgiveness of sin and the faith that on the last day, our soul and a new heavenly body would be united to live in paradise forever with Him. Now, that leads us to ask questions as to what happens immediately after our passing.

## One with God

Based on the truth which is only found in the Bible, our soul-spirit will immediately be in heaven, united with Jesus and our loved ones, if we are free from serious sin. After the second coming of Jesus, as revealed to us in the book of Revelation, we will be united with a new heavenly body.

It is difficult for our human nature to understand how we pass from earthly existence to eternal life, but that is the promise of Jesus. That is where our faith points—an eternal life of perfect happiness.

Is it worth looking forward to, or would you rather put aside His promise and for the time being not have Jesus be a daily part of your life? If that choice is made, remember that this life is temporary and at some time will end. Eternity is forever. St James told us, "What is your life? It is even a vapor that appears for a little time and then vanishes away" (James 4:14).

*"He said to them, 'Strive to enter through the narrow gate, for many, I say to you, will seek to enter and will not be able'" (Luke 13:24).*

# The Pathway

*The narrow gate*

Getting to heaven is not automatic. A person can

lead a life they might consider to be righteous and therefore believe that the conditions for salvation have been met. No, that is not correct. It is not what one *thinks* righteousness is, it is what the Bible teaches us: giving yourself completely to Jesus, accepting Him as your personal Savior, and believing in and obeying all His teachings. *That is the pathway to heaven.* Jesus is waiting for you to come to Him, ask for His forgiveness for past wrongdoings, and start your new life with Him by your side. What are you waiting for? Get moving before it is too late.

*"In My Father's house are many mansions; if it were not so, I would have told you. I go to prepare a place for you" (John 14:2).*

## The Questions

I believe that most people at one time or another have wondered about their promised heavenly existence.

- Will we know and be with our loved ones?
- Will there truly be no pain or suffering?

- Where will we live?
- What will we do?

The questions go on and on. Where do we find the answers? The true answers to those questions and all others concerning heaven can only be found in the Bible. Just think of where those words came from and the divine power of each one. The Bible is not a book that you just scan through. It is a book where every word has a sacred and eternal meaning.

*Welcome to Paradise*

# No More Pain

God revealed a vivid description of the end of times to the apostle John during his imprisonment on the Greek island of Patmos: "God will wipe away every tear from their eyes; there shall be no more death, nor sorrow, nor crying. There shall be no more pain, for the former things have passed away" (Revelation 21:4).

# Animals In Heaven?

I recently was asked a question about family pets and other animals being in heaven. I go back to what I previously said, and that is, all we know about heaven is what God has revealed to us in the Book of Truth, and that He does numerous times.

> The wolf and the lamb shall graze together;
>  the lion shall eat straw like the ox,
>  and dust shall be the serpent's food.
> They shall not hurt or destroy

in all my holy mountain,"

says the Lord (Isaiah 65:25).

I never doubted pets' heavenly existence, for they were created by God for the pleasure of mankind. "All flesh shall see the salvation of God" (Luke 3:6).

*Animals living together peacefully in paradise*

I am sure that some people do not have an immediate concern about heaven. They would rather live a relativistic life of being a free spirit with self-justification for now and be concerned about their final destiny later. What a mistake that could be! In Matthew 24:36, Jesus told us "Of that day and hour no one knows, not even the angels of heaven, but My Father only." Do you still want to take a chance on your destiny? If so, good luck. Sometimes it takes a wake-up call to realize how temporary our existence is.

# 2

# What Is Heaven Like?

Do not waste your time searching for what people think heaven will be like, for Scripture tells us that all things will be made new and beyond the comprehension of humanity. Accept the Word of God, have faith, and strive for righteousness—the golden ticket to heaven.

For those who doubt its reality, I suggest getting a Bible and, for starters, to meditate on the following:

*"In My Father's house are many mansions; if it were not so, I would have told you. I go to prepare a place for you" (John 14:2).*

*"The Lord will deliver me from every evil work and preserve me for His heavenly kingdom" (2 Timothy 4:18).*

*"I say to you, I will not drink of this fruit of the vine from now on until that day when I drink it new with you in My Father's kingdom" (Matthew 26:29).*

## Paradise

*"Remember me."*

One of the most powerful statements referring to the

existence of heaven came from Jesus while on the cross. It was when one of the two criminals also being crucified acknowledged Jesus as the Christ and asked to be remembered when Jesus was in heaven. Because of his acceptance and belief, Jesus told him that that day he would be with Him in His heavenly home.

*"He said to Jesus, 'Lord, remember me when You come into Your kingdom.' And Jesus said to him, 'Assuredly, I say to you, today you will be with Me in Paradise'" (Luke 23:42–43).*

The Bible tells us that heaven is a glorious eternal existence that always was and always will be. Living there should be the goal of all humanity, for our citizenship is of heaven. Earth is just a stopover, and we are here on a temporary visa that will expire at a time unknown to us. The reason for our existence on earth and not in paradise is that our humanity has been corrupted by the willful disobedience of Adam and Eve to God's command. Their punishment was expulsion from paradise and therefore what never was intended to be, namely sin and death, became the reality for all. However, God, out of His unconditional love, gave us the gift of free will to choose righteousness, which is our heavenly passport to our eternal home. Unfortunately, that goal will not be achieved by everyone. The reason being is sin. If righteousness is not the choice made during our humanity, our passports will be voided and entrance into heaven denied.

We all have heard the biblical scripture that you reap what you sow. Regrettably, there will be instances during our lifetime when what we sow will not be from righteousness. God realizes that is because of our human nature, so through His grace, He has given us the great gift of forgiveness. Nonetheless, forgiveness should not be taken lightly. It requires remorse and a sincere effort to avoid repetition. Can a person be a sinner and still be saved? Yes, he or she can, and that is because of the unconditional love God has for all humanity. If one is sorry, asks for forgiveness, and tries to change his ways, he will be forgiven.

*Forgiveness*

# 3

# Can People Change?

Saul's life is an excellent example of a person's character transformation and reversal of ideology. This took place during the early stages of Christianity. Saul was a Jewish-Roman citizen born in Tarsus, Turkey—a part of the Roman Empire. He was a devout Jew who followed without question the Jewish beliefs, traditions, and practices to the fullest and therefore despised all those who did not, especially the followers of Jesus. The fundamental reason was that Jesus claimed to be the Son of God and the Messiah. Saul could not accept those claims, regardless of the numerous miracles performed by Jesus and witnessed by thousands of people. Jesus's response to those who did not believe was, "If I do not do the works of My Father, do not believe Me; but if I do, though you do not believe Me, believe the works, that you may know and believe that the Father is in Me, and I in Him" (John 10:37–38). His response is the same to us today.

## He Didn't Understand

Saul's perspective was to not believe that to be possible. How could the son of a carpenter be the Messiah or claim to be the Son of God? To Saul, Jesus and His disciples were evil people who were preaching lies and filling the Jews' heads with objectionable information contrary to Jewish law and tradition. Saul further believed that the followers of Jesus formed an undesirable "cult" that had no place in Jewish society, that they must be harshly dealt with by prosecution, imprisonment, or even death. In reality, Saul was the evil one, not Jesus and His followers, but his mindset was about to change.

Shortly after the crucifixion and death of Jesus, Saul

was traveling on the road to Damascus to a location where he and his companions expected to find a group of Jesus's followers conducting a service. His mission was to disband the assembly and bring the participants back to Israel, where they would be imprisoned or worse.

That was not to be for, suddenly, a bright, blinding light caused Saul to fall to the ground, startled and fearful. He then heard a voice say "Saul, Saul, why are you persecuting Me?" An awed and frightened Saul then asked, "Who are you?" And the voice said, "I am Jesus, whom you are persecuting" (Acts 9:4–5).

*Paul was blinded by a bright light from heaven*

Saul was dumbfounded, terrified, and greatly bewildered by all that was taking place. He was probably thinking, *Is this happening or am I dreaming?* Yes, it was happening. Jesus then told Saul to go into the city and meet with Ananias, a disciple of Jesus. Saul did. He was baptized by Ananias, and his conversion to Christianity immediately took place. He was no longer a persecutor of Jesus but a believer who dedicated the remainder of his life as a missionary to gentiles throughout the Roman Empire. His new life mission was now to preach the gospel of Jesus and establish new Christian communities. He did so faithfully, constantly facing hardships or imprisonment. In the process, he brought many thousands of converts to the truth—Christianity.

His name was no longer Saul but Paulus, a Roman name meaning Paul. It was because of his unwavering belief in Jesus that he was unjustly convicted in Rome of sedition charges and sentenced by Nero to be executed. Before his execution, he wrote to Timothy, a disciple, and said: "I have fought the good fight, I have finished the race, I have kept the faith. Finally, there is laid up for me the crown of righteousness" (2 Timothy 4:7–8).

*A crown of righteousness*

## Righteousness for All

Jesus saw special something in Paul, as he does in all people. He does not expect us to be gifted preachers of the gospel as Paul was, but He does expect us to live a life of righteousness and thus earn our eternal inheritance, which is available to all humanity.

> Walk in the Spirit, and you shall not fulfill the lust of the flesh. For the flesh lusts against the Spirit, and the Spirit against the flesh; and these are contrary to one another, so that you do not do the things that you wish. But if you are led by the Spirit, you are not under the law.
>
> Now the works of the flesh are evident, which are: adultery, fornication, uncleanness, lewdness, idolatry, sorcery, hatred, contentions, jealousies, outbursts of wrath, selfish ambitions, dissensions, heresies, envy, murders, drunkenness, revelries, and the like; of which I tell you beforehand, just as I also told you in time past, that those who practice such things will not inherit the kingdom of God.
>
> —Galatians 5:16–21

Unfortunately, the misuse of the magnificent gift of free will might result in choices of unrighteousness, causing our crown of glory to never be received. It does not have to be that way, for if we believe, ask for forgiveness, and sincerely try to remove the stain of sin from our soul, the heavenly light of salvation will guide us home through the grace of God.

# 4

# What's the Truth?

"If a wicked man turns from all his sins which he has committed, keeps all My statutes, and does what is lawful and right, he shall surely live; he shall not die. None of the transgressions which he has committed shall be remembered against him; because of the righteousness which he has done, he shall live. Do I have any pleasure at all that the wicked should die?" says the Lord God, "and not that he should turn from his ways and live?"

—Ezekiel 18:21–23

Ezekiel was a prophet of God who lived around 598 BC. Being a prophet, his words were the words of God, given to him for all people to hear and abide by. The previously quoted passage should be considered a statement of hope needed by mankind both then and now. The spoken words came directly from God through Ezekiel. How much more proof would a doubter need? Almighty God, our creator, is never to be doubted and always to be believed and obeyed. None of His words are to be changed or modified to seek an individual's desired meaning.

## Seek the Truth

We always should seek the truth. There are many answers to everything imageable, justifiably so. However, the question then arises as to the objectivity of the answer. We want to know if it is true or something concocted to influence beliefs and actions. That is a good question and, in most cases, should need verification before acceptance, except when the answer comes directly from the Word of God.

The gift of life is God's covenant made with humanity to be found in the greatest book ever written, the Holy Bible. Read it and your life will be forever changed.

# What Is the Bible?

The Bible is God's master plan for our salvation and a road map for a life of righteousness.

> I do not receive honor from men. But I know you, that you do not have the love of God in you. I have come in My Father's name, and you do not receive Me; if another comes in his own name, him you will receive. How can you believe, who receive honor from one another, and do not seek the honor that *comes* from the only God?
>
> —John 5:41–45

*The apostle John, the author of Revelation*

As with any historical work, regardless of its topic, the questions should be asked:

1. Who is the author?
2. When was it written?
3. Is there substantial evidence to prove its creditability?
4. What is its purpose?

When it comes to the Bible or other religious works, some have adopted an antireligious attitude and have no interest in discovering the truth. In my book, *Believe in Me for I Am the Way*, I state, "Unfortunately, there are those who dispute the Holy Bible and question its accuracy. Is that because of its religious nature? Is it that today there is a need to question everything religious?" I believe so.

Yet when the same people read a nonreligious book, acceptance of the written content is usually not questioned. For example, they read a historical book about well-known world leaders of the past, who lived thousands of years before the birth of Jesus. Their existence and the minute details of their rules are not questioned. Why is that? The obvious reason is because of the authentic documentation of the facts available. Yet when it comes to the gospels—even with the written words of people who witnessed Jesus's preaching, miracles, crucifixion, death, and resurrection—there still is rejection. It breaks down to the lack of having an open mind and an objective attitude. Why not let the facts speak for themselves?

*Witnesses of Jesus's miracles*

# Use the Objective Approach

This past year, I was invited to be a guest speaker at a well-known college in New England, where my daughter was teaching a psychology class. It was requested that the topics of discussion center around the meaning of religion and spirituality, and their influence on life in general. The class consisted of about thirty-five students and because of COVID-19, the discussion was held as a Zoom session. Quite frankly, I was pleasantly surprised by the students' quest for religious knowledge. They, like most younger people I have spoken with, were seeking answers; and as we well know, there certainly are numerous answers available to whatever their questions or concerns might be. I believe that seeking the truth regardless of where it leads should always be the intention. That, of course, requires:

- knowing where to find the truth,
- always taking an objective path regarding the material available, and

- not following a relativistic way of molding the findings to suit one's individual needs.

Unfortunately, the objective approach is not how it always happens. Today, answers are usually expected immediately and, as we know, can result in a less than complete investigative process. The result is that the approach can end in a limited search usually trending toward a subjective conclusion. In other words, suit the personal wishes and no further information is needed.

As the discussion went on, it became apparent that a moral order in society was universally accepted but how it was established and practiced was accomplished in more of an individual manner. Unfortunately, that is a universal norm throughout our society, regardless of age or status. We discussed the need for a structured approach from an accepted religious point of view, not one based on individuality but on a solid spiritual foundation given to us by God for all humanity to live by. By doing so, the meaning of life and all it has to offer will then become apparent. Life should not be about how *I* should live but how *we* should live.

The attentiveness and questions asked by the students showed me that these young men and women were seeking answers and were willing to take the extra steps necessary to find them. It also pointed out that their professor's method of instruction was a major contributor in helping each one to realize the *God-given* ability they possessed and how to release that capability and intelligence by opening the floodgate of knowledge that is available to all. It is like the old exercise axiom that if you don't use it, you will lose it. I pray that their quest for knowledge will lead them to the answers they seek, namely truth and righteousness—the only way of life that can change the world from the evil that has engulfed its essence.

Always seek the truth from an objective point of view, regardless of the direction it might take. Too many times subjectivity becomes the key factor in the acceptance or rejection of something, thus resulting in a distorted and unfounded conclusion. Never let the truth be influenced by the desire for it to suit personal needs according to preconceived opinions.

# The Facts about the Bible

- What is the Bible?
- Who are the authors?
- Why should their writings be accepted as the truth?

The Holy Bible is God's master plan for the salvation of mankind. It consists of seventy-three books or letters and is the undeniable Word of God. It explains and instructs us how to achieve righteousness on earth, which in turn establishes the pathway to eternal salvation.

The Old Testament includes forty-six books, and the New Testament is comprised of twenty-seven books and letters, all substantiated and proven to be the infallible words of God.

They have been validated by the discovery of the 2,000-year-old Dead Sea Scrolls, found intact in caves along the Israeli shores of the Dead Sea. What is amazing is that experts were able to reconstruct around 950 different manuscripts, verifying their legitimacy.

More than 5,700 Greek manuscripts of the New Testament writings were also found, and by detailed examination, 99 percent of the original text was reconstructed and proven to be accurate beyond a reasonable doubt. Amazing, isn't it? How can anyone claim the Bible is fiction?

The Bible can be classified as its own library consisting of nonfiction, history, poetry, and literature; but most important of all, it's *the absolute truth never to be added to or have words taken away from.*

*Historical scrolls*

This magnificent testament of sacred writings has a personality of being unique because it is the direct Word of God, given to humanity through His chosen prophets.

# 5

# The Greatest Story Ever Told

There are so many terrific books in the Bible, but the greatest story ever told has to be the first book about the creation of the world and humanity, the book of Genesis.

"In the beginning God created the heavens and the earth. The earth was without form, and void; and darkness was on the face of the deep. And the Spirit of God was hovering over the face of the waters. … Then God said, "Let there be a firmament in the midst of the waters, and let it divide the waters from the waters." Thus God made the firmament, and divided the waters which were under the firmament from the waters which were above the firmament; and it was so. And God called the firmament Heaven" (Genesis 1:1–2, 6–8).

What is most amazing is that God, through His infinite omnipotence, verbally created the world, sun, stars, day, night, oceans, dry earth, and all else on the face of the planet in six days. He then created the first human inhabitants, Adam and Eve. It was their disobedience to God's command not to eat the fruit from the Tree of Knowledge that resulted in what was never intended to be—sin, expulsion from paradise, and death for all generations until the end of times.

> Then God said, "Let Us make man in Our image, according to Our likeness; let them have dominion over the fish of the sea, over the birds of the air, and over the cattle, over all the earth and over every creeping thing that creeps on the earth." So God created man in His *own* image; in the image of God He created him; male and female He created them.
>
> — Genesis 1:26–27

Go back to the verse "Let us make man in Our image, according to Our likeness." Our soul is blessed with the spiritual DNA of God. Therefore, our bodies are His spiritual vessel, possessing the gift of free will and filled with the overflowing love of our divine creator. Think of that every time the darkness of evil tries to take control of your actions.

*Adam and Eve, the first humans*

## We Always Have a Choice

I have been a prison minister for the past fifteen years, and during that time, I have been asked many times by inmates that if God knows everything, why didn't He stop Adam and Eve from disobeying Him? The answer to that question is two words: *free will*. God, out of extreme love for His creation, gave them and all following human beings that divine gift. How it is used will be one of the determining factors of where our eternity will be spent.

Will it be eternal salvation or eternal destruction? That is entirely up to each one of us. Live a life of righteousness on earth and spend eternity in heaven. Of course we will sin. All human beings are sinners, but those sins can be forgiven if we are sorry and ask our Lord for forgiveness through repentance.

*"If we confess our sins, He is faithful and just to forgive us our sins and to cleanse us from all unrighteousness" (1 John 1:9).*

# 6

# This Gift of Life

The world experienced a terrifying COVID-19 global pandemic from 2020 to 2022, responsible for more than six million deaths worldwide. Fortunately, vaccines are now available, and this battle against the disease will eventually be won. I say battle instead of war because as depressing as it sounds, there will be many other battles fought for the salvation of humanity. After that will come the signs of the times and the end of the age.

> Jesus answered and said to them: "You will hear of wars and rumors of wars. See that you are not troubled; for all *these things* must come to pass, but the end is not yet.
> For nation will rise against nation, and kingdom against kingdom. And there will be famines, pestilences, and

earthquakes in various places. All these *are* the beginning of sorrows."

—Matthew 24:4–8

It is, however, not all doom and gloom. That is not the way God wants us to live; he wants us to enjoy the gift of life and, through His generosity, all it has to offer. We can enjoy our ever-growing faith, hope, and knowledge that through righteousness on earth, our crown of glory is awaiting us. God wants us to always be aware that life on earth is temporary, and that at a time unknown to us, our earthly presence will end. Then what? Is that the end? We believers know it is not the end, for it is just the beginning of a new, everlasting life, free from all the personal difficulties and challenges of our humanity.

## Don't Quit!

It is so easy to just give up when things appear to be deteriorating and the dark cloud of hopelessness seems to be engulfing one's being. It would be so effortless to just surrender to whatever is going to take place. That is the easy approach to take. Just step aside and do not let the temporary false feeling of relief saturate oneself only to have the helpless feelings repeated again and again. No, that is not the attitude to have. Accept what God has to offer; that is not defeat but the strength and will to face the difficulty and the courage to win the battle. Once that takes place, the shadow of darkness will be conquered and the brightness of victory will lead us on through our trials.

*Jesus conquered darkness once and for all*

The Bible has so many exceptional stories about not surrendering to injustice but having the courage to stand up for what is right, regardless of the consequences. One such biblical story takes place in Persia around 478 BC, which we can read about in the book of Esther.

---

# Esther

Esther was a Jewish immigrant to Persia, and after the death of her mother and father, she was raised by Mordecai, her uncle. Life was not easy for them, for the Jews were considered to be beneath the Persians and a threat to the empire. Many wanted them eliminated.

Ahasuerus, King of Persia, and his queen, Vashti, resided in the capital city of Shushan, where he ruled over his vast empire of 126 provinces covering approximately 2,775 miles. Persia was a great conquering power, having Jewish settlements in all the provinces, and that was of concern to the Persians, who were plotting the mass extermination of God's chosen people.

King Ahasuerus's wife Queen Vashti had little if any

interest in the plight of the Jewish people. She was a very selfish, independent woman who enjoyed the power her title gave her, even though at times that power would be overstepped to accommodate her wishes. That is exactly what took place when the king requested her presence at a royal palace banquet. If the king requested your presence and that request was ignored, the results could be devastating, and it was for Queen Vashti. Her disobedience and overbearing independence resulted in losing her royal position and all the advantages of being the queen that came with it. Consequently, the king banished her and decided to select a new queen—a young Jewish girl named Esther.

Soon after Esther became queen, she became aware of an edict issued by the king allowing for the extermination of all the Jews living in the empire. Saving her people was now in her hands. She planned to approach the king directly without going through the established protocol of first requesting an audience. By doing so, she risked the consequences that direction might bring. Even though she was queen, she was required to follow the strict protocol of the crown. The king's love and respect toward his new queen were obvious, and even though Esther violated regal procedures, the king canceled the extermination edict upon Esther's request and issued a royal decree assuring the protection of all Jews throughout the empire.

*Esther and the king*

It was that poor little Jewish girl Esther who prevented the genocide of the Jewish people more than two thousand years ago. Her love for her people took priority over her well-being.

God had a plan for their salvation, and Esther was His choice to see that it successfully took place.

---

# Does God Have a Plan?

We often wonder if God has a plan for us. Yes, He does. Be patient, have courage, and believe, and it will be revealed to you according to His timetable. Unfortunately, many in today's society are on the fast track, seeking and expecting immediate answers. That is not always the best approach. Slow down, ask God to calm your mind, and use that mighty gift of wisdom in the decision-making process.

The following prayer by Orin Crain titled "Slow Me Down, Lord" says it all.

> *Ease the pounding of my heart by the quieting of my mind. Steady my hurried pace with a vision of the eternal reach of time.*
>
> *Give me, amidst the confusion of my day, the calmness of the everlasting hills. Break the tension of my nerves*

*and muscles with the soothing music of the singing streams that live in my memory.*

*Help me to know the magical, restorative power of sleep. Teach me the art of taking minute vacations, of slowing down to look at a flower, to chat with a friend, to pet a dog, to read a few lines of a good book.*

*Remind me each day of the fable of the hare and the tortoise, that I may know that the race is not always to the swift; that there is more to life than increasing its speed.*

*Let me look upward into the branches of the towering trees and know that they grow tall because they grow slowly and well.*

*Slow me down, Lord, and inspire me to send my roots deep into the soil of life's enduring values, that I may grow towards the stars of my great destiny.*

*Amen*

# 7

# When All Seems Lost

Moses is credited as being the author of the first five books of the Old Testament, the words personally given to him by Almighty God. Like Moses, the authors of the remaining forty-one books were also prophets instructed by God to preach His word to all people. When a prophet spoke, it was the words revealed to them from God.

Moses was a Jew, born into Egyptian captivity and living in a slave ghetto. The Jews were subject to the harsh rule of the Egyptians and were primarily exposed to the rigid physical labor of making bricks, used for numerous building projects throughout the empire.

Over the years, the Jewish population grew substantially, and that concerned the Egyptian ruler, Pharaoh Seti. He feared that their growing strength in numbers could eventually result in a rebellion and their leaving Egypt. If that took place, who then would do the slave labor of brickmaking? Consequently, the Pharaoh issued an edict stating that all Jewish male infants were to be killed as a method of controlling their population and thus reducing the possibility of a future insurrection.

## A Mother's Love

The infant Moses was spared death by his mother placing him in a basket and putting it among the reeds along the shoreline of the Nile River. She hoped that the basket would be found, and her child would thus escape death as decreed by the Pharaoh.

Her wish came to fruition for the basket was found by a member of the royal family, Princess Hatshepsut, who, out of extreme love, adopted him as her son and named him Moses, meaning "to be pulled out from the water." Moses was educated in the royal palace and brought up as an Egyptian. He eventually became the master builder of Egypt.

The Egyptians were not a monotheistic society, for they worshiped many gods. To name a few, Amun-Ra the Hidden One, Osiris the King of the Living, and Ra, the god of the sun. Moses being a Jew, gradually began to accept the Jewish monotheistic faith of believing in the one and only true God.

*Moses, the deliverer*

His life was forever changed when trying to protect a

Jew who was being assaulted by an Egyptian for refusing an extortion payment. It was during the encounter with Moses, that the Egyptian was accidentally killed, and according to Egyptian law that was an automatic death sentence for the accused. Realizing what the unjust consequences for his actions would be, he then fled Egypt and lived as a nomad in the desert with his father-in-law, Reuel, his wife Zipporah, and his sons.

It was not until he was eighty years old that God openly spoke to him with instructions to go back to Egypt, free His chosen people from slavery, and bring them to the promised land. That he agreed to do, but not without serious concerns about his ability to do so.

*"Come now, therefore, and I will send you to Pharaoh that you may bring My people, the children of Israel, out of Egypt" (Exodus 3:10).*

Did you ever feel that a goal you wanted to achieve presented too many obstacles and therefore was beyond your capability? I am sure you have. We all have. As Moses realized, spiritual assistance is sometimes needed, and if your wishes are what God wants you to do, with His help, they will be achieved.

## How Do You Get His Help?

The answer to that question is through prayer, seeking righteousness first, being patient, and in time all else will fall into place. Unfortunately, most of us are by nature impatient and expect immediate answers. God does not work that way. As stated in 2 Peter 3:8: "Beloved, do not forget this one thing, that with the Lord one day is as a thousand years, and a thousand years as one day." That does not mean that your prayers will not be answered for what we would think is an eternity. What it does mean is to be patient and persistent in your request. They will be answered and usually in a way that was never expected. The pathway to accomplishment is to follow the guidance of God wherever it may take you. He is not going to speak directly to you as He did to Moses, but through the power of His Holy Spirit, the direction to take will become clear.

Just have faith, trust, and most of all belief.

> *"Have I not commanded you? Be strong and of good courage; do not be afraid, nor be dismayed, for the Lord your God is with you wherever you go" (Joshua 1:9).*

---

# Failure Can Be a Key

Frequently in life, it sometimes takes failure to achieve success. That can be exceedingly difficult for most people to understand, especially for the person experiencing it. I believe that the majority of those reading this book will agree that failure can usually be related to making poor choices. Once we realize that God is needed to guide us, and we seek His help, then and only then will the twilight of a new beginning ignite the darkness of failure. It might be an entirely different direction than expected but when it does take place, it will be God leading us to accomplish what will then, become the cornerstone of our achievements.

*God knows our path before we are born,*
*just like Moses's*

I never thought that I would be a prison minister, bringing the Word of God to the incarcerated or that I in my old age would write three books about Christianity. What a change from the stressful everyday business world. God works in strange ways. I am sure He always wanted to have a spiritual dialogue with me, but unfortunately, my agenda was focused elsewhere.

It was while having dinner with close friends that our discussion changed unexpectantly from everyday topics to religion and the back seat it had taken in our daily lives. It was a friend's following words that changed my life direction: "Did you ever think of being a prison minister?" Those nine spoken words were a beacon of light putting me on a new life course—God's course. That was part of God's plan for me to accept or reject. I did not realize it at the time but after considerable soul searching, I decided to move forward with God's plan for which I will forever be grateful. Be patient, listen for his word, and through prayer, you will make the right choices in life.

## Fight for What Is Good

When all seems lost and nothing appears to be moving in the right direction, despair is setting in and the feeling of failure engulfs your soul, do not give up. When you want to give up, you are missing what God has to offer. Fight for what is good. Have courage and do not surrender to the evil of unrighteousness. You are not alone; you are in the hands of God. He will provide you with spiritual strength when you need it most.

Stop feeling sorry for yourself. Seek help from God, your divine healer. He is the person who never has and never will give up on you and does not expect you to succumb to the gloom of self-defeat. He has been waiting to be acknowledged as your creator and for you to ask for His help and guidance. Once that takes place, you will experience the dense fog of failure begin to ebb and open a pathway to a new dawn.

# 8

# What Really Matters?

Too often, we go through life stumbling, not knowing what we genuinely want. We say we know, but do we? If you answer that question from an objective point of view, I believe the truth will prevail.

> *"Fear not, for I am with you;*
> *Be not dismayed, for I am your God.*
> *I will strengthen you,*
> *Yes, I will help you,*
> *I will uphold you with My righteous right*
> *hand" (Isaiah 41:10).*

An example is living life with excessive emphasis on temporal gains. Once that takes place, it usually results in a serious decline in spiritual values. Let us think of it as a two-sided balance scale. One side represents materialistic values and the other spiritual. When both are pursued equally, success can be guaranteed.

Sadly, the balance between the two is not always achievable, and that is because of the driving material desire for more. When that happens, we push God out of our lives, sometimes without even realizing that it is taking place.

*Make a change*

*"We do not look at the things which are seen, but at the things which are not seen. For the things which are seen are temporary, but the things*

*which are not seen are eternal" (2 Corinthians 4:18).*

---

## You Can't Keep Any of It

We all have heard it said that "you can't take it with you." How true that is. Once we leave for our final destination, all material valuables will remain behind. They are meaningless. The poorest and richest are equal in the eyes of God. However, how one's wealth was acquired and used will be factors regarding final judgment and the passport to where the ever after will be spent. I have mentioned numerous times that there is nothing wrong with achieving and enjoying the benefits of one's efforts if they are acquired through righteousness and acknowledged as gifts from God. How unfortunate it is for many that those temporal accomplishments sometimes take priority over spiritual values and become the choice of importance. That holds true for all people, regardless of their life status, poverty or wealth. It is not the amount of money or the personal possessions acquired that matter, for the homeless person's meager possessions, as well as the rich man's wealth, will be left behind.

*"Where your treasure is, there your heart will be also" (Luke 12:34).*

Jesus told us that if righteousness is our chosen way of life, a heavenly reward will be awaiting us. If the achievement of wealth becomes the primary goal, the benefits of God's kingdom will not be one's priority and could result in the loss of reaping the triumph and splendor of our heavenly crown of glory.

*"What will it profit a man if he gains the whole world, and loses his own soul?" (Mark 8:36).*

## It's All Temporal

Temporal possessions are just that, temporal meaning earthly or materialistic. What is important is that we do not let the process of acquiring material gains become the cause of a spiraling spiritual downfall. Use the gift of free will to choose goodness first and God will not let you down. Sometimes the material possessions sought after will come at a price that takes precedence over what truly matters, namely saving one's soul. If that is the case, watch out, for you are being led down the road to eternal disaster. I cannot emphasize enough the fact that our time on earth is determined by a limited number of years, whereas eternity cannot be measured for it is forever. So, what does this all mean? We all want to achieve and, hopefully, have what will bring us some measure of happiness on earth. Is that what God wants for us? Yes, He does if it is brought to pass through righteousness. Our soul was created in the image and likeness of God, which means every human being has God's spiritual DNA. Use it wisely and do not succumb to the evil stranglehold of sinful temptations.

# 9

# Feeling Helpless?

There are two perceptions of life to consider when trying to understand the concept of existence. One is temporal and the other eternal, one leads to euphoria and the other everlasting despair. Either is our decision to make. Humanity is temporary and eternity is permanent. The latter is strictly dependent on the life choices we make during our brief stopover on earth. Serious attention should be given as to how that can be. Do you have control over your destiny? The answer is an emphatic yes.

A contributing factor to damnation is the misuse of free will. Free will gives us the ability to make individual choices that eventually will engrave the seal of our chosen destiny on our souls. That gift formulates the cornerstone for the direction of our life on earth and, more importantly, the achievement of reaching our eternal residence. Free will is a major ingredient in finding our way home.

## You Decide

All human beings are given the divine gift of free will, putting each of us on the highest plane of creation. Free will is the unhindered ability to choose between different possible courses of action. Of course, this does not hold for people who are unable to fully exercise their decision-making process. Examples are mental illness or the limitation of physical freedom. However, if the person does have the cognitive ability, the spiritual inheritance of free will is always present. How we use that gift is the determining factor as to the temporal existence we will experience and, most important of all, the grand prize we believers seek—salvation.

Do not be deceived, God is not mocked; for whatever a man sows, that he will also reap. For he who sows to his flesh will of the flesh reap corruption, but he who sows to the Spirit will of the Spirit reap everlasting life. And let us not grow weary while doing good, for in due season we shall reap if we do not lose heart.

— Galatians 6:7–9

*Decision-making*

# Be Prepared

Our life on earth is an unknown journey through time. It might end anywhere from infancy to old age, and this end is influenced by circumstances, many of which we have little or no control over, such as illness, accidents, or natural disasters. When it is time to move on to our endless closing chapter, our life of immortality, it will be God's indisputable judgment as to where that life will be spent. So now is the time to get it right with Him. Without question, the whereabouts will be determined by our humanity of goodness or lack of. I like to think of our terrestrial residence as a stopover on the final leg to a promised perpetual, joyous existence in paradise.

*"You do not know what will happen tomorrow. For what is your life? It is even a vapor that appears for a little time and then vanishes away"* (James 4:14).

Being prepared is not only about saving oneself, for trying to lead a life of goodness will not only bring the gift of salvation, but that direction will certainly affect the lives of others. Most importantly, you will be following Jesus's command to be His disciple and to influence others by your words and actions.

# Change Is Not Easy

The more people are set in their ways, the less they believe that change is needed. Frequently, the question "Why do I need to change?" arises from the incarcerated men I talk with. The obvious answer is if you do not want to spend the rest of your life in prison, you need change. More importantly, where do you want to spend eternity? There are only two locations, heaven or hell.

During my many years serving God as a prison minister, I have met more than a few inmates who felt that way and asked, "Why should I change? I do not have any future to look forward to, and nobody I know cares whether I change my ways or not." *Jesus cares.* He gave His life so that we and all humanity would have a pathway to salvation and, through His teachings, a life of righteousness on earth.

# Your Value

This reminds me of the story "You Are Still Priceless."

A well-known speaker started his seminar by holding up a $20 bill. In the room of 200, he asked, Who would like this $20 bill?

Hands started going up. He said, I am going to give this $20 to one of you but first, let me do this. He then proceeded to crumple the dollar bill up. He then asked, who still wants it? Still the hands were up in the air.

Well, he replied, what if I do this? And he dropped it on the floor and started to grind it into the floor with his shoe. He picked it up, now all crumpled and dirty. Now, who wants it? Still, the hands went into the air.

My friends, you have all learned a very valuable lesson. No matter what I did to the money, you still wanted it because it did not decrease in value. It was still worth $20.

Many times in our lives, we are dropped, crumpled, and ground into the dirt by decisions we make and the circumstances that come our way. We feel as though we are worthless. But no matter what has happened or what will happen, you will never lose your value. Dirty or clean, crumpled or finely creased, *you are still priceless.*

—Unknown author, "You Are Still Priceless." www.godsbibletruth.com/priceless.html

That is the way God sees us, regardless of our past actions, for He is a forgiving God who loves us unconditionally. He wants us to be happy, to look at life having a positive attitude, to seek righteousness first, and to put a sincere effort into whatever honorable endeavors we choose. Our worldly presence will always include emotional fluctuations, some more severe than others. Learning how to handle them and getting through the difficult times is paramount to ever achieving a feeling of contentment and peace of mind. Our terrestrial voyage is temporary, and without righteousness in our life, the contentment and peace we seek can never be permanent.

# Steps to Happiness

## *Everyone knows*

- ✓ You cannot be all things to all people.
- ✓ You cannot do all things at once.
- ✓ You cannot do all things equally well.
- ✓ You cannot do all things better than everyone else.
- ✓ Your humanity is showing just like everyone else's.

## *So*

- ✓ You have to find out who you are and be that.
- ✓ You have to decide what comes first and do it.
- ✓ You have to discover your strengths and use them.
- ✓ You have to learn not to compete with others because no one else is in the contest of being you.

## *Then*

- ✓ You will have learned to accept your own uniqueness.
- ✓ You will have learned to set priorities and make decisions.
- ✓ You will have learned to live with your limitations.

✓ You will have learned to give yourself the respect that is due.

"Seek first the kingdom of God and His righteousness, and all these things shall be added to you. Therefore do not worry about tomorrow, for tomorrow will worry about its own things. Sufficient for the day is its own trouble" (Matthew 6:33–34).

On the wall of my doctor's office reception area is a plaque with the following inspiring quotation: "Life is not made up of worrying about when the storm will pass; it is about learning to dance in the rain."

What an encouraging message of acceptance and of the need to move forward.

Being human, we will be confronted with physical and possibly mental ailments during our lifetime that will raise the "why me" question. This can lead to depression and a despondent, hopeless attitude. In most cases, the "storm" is not anyone's fault. Good and bad things happen.

## Trust and Believe

In the book of Ecclesiastes, the prophet King Solomon pointed out that life is not perfect and that imperfections are common to human beings. They are and always will be part of our life. During the process of coping with whatever the storm is, the "why me" attitude does not have to be the question asked because through hope and trust in God, that negative mindset can be replaced with a positive and confident approach. The effortless way out is to surrender, but it does not have to be that way.

67

*Just trust and believe in Him.*

*"Come to Me, all you who labor and are heavy laden, and I will give you rest" (Matthew 11:28).*

Too often we go through life having a disproportionate and needless concern about the present and future state of circumstances over which we have little or no control. I know that I fall in that category and, more than likely, so do most people. We all want to achieve various objectives in life, and that is good, but we should not let that which is beyond our control direct the course of our lives.

Matthew 6:33 tells us to first plan to make His kingdom the most important objective, and through seeking righteousness first, all else will eventually fall in its appropriate place. That does not mean we should put aside our expectations and eagerness to achieve our ambitions. No, not at all. We certainly should plan for the future, and by believing in the Almighty, all else will be set in motion according to His plan. However, unless we have complete faith and trust in Him, a course of righteousness will never take priority and could lead to destructive results.

*Get on the boat with Jesus*

In my book *Navigating through the Storms of a Christian Life*, I attempt to bring out the need of Jesus by the following comparison.

> Life without Jesus is like being on a boat without a rudder in a violent and powerful storm. The boat goes this way and that way depending on the wind, waves, and currents. No steady direction can be maintained, and disaster is always present. When we bring Jesus into our lives, our course of righteousness becomes clear.

He is our rudder, and through His grace, the storms of life can be confronted and defeated.

# 10

# What Is Righteous-ness?

Jesus came to us having both a human and divine nature. His humanity was one of righteousness and His divine nature was and always will be the second person of the Holy Trinity, God the Son. Being a Christian means living life according to Jesus's teachings. That seems to be pretty straightforward, but it is not because other than Jesus, all human beings have been and will continue to be sinners by words, thoughts, or actions.

Before we move on, let us look at the meaning of righteousness and how its influence on life will be a major factor in achieving a more purposeful temporal and eternal existence. As we read the Bible, the word "righteousness" is mentioned more than 530 times. I would think that points out its importance.

The word "righteousness" has both a human and spiritual meaning. From the values of humanity, it can be considered as the quality of being morally true or justifiable. Spiritually, though, righteousness is the quality of being right in the eyes of God in character, thoughts, words, and deeds. It is my opinion that the values of humanity infer a personal meaning designed to fit the individual's needs. For a Christian, righteousness is acting in accord with divine law and the laws of man. Divine laws are the laws of God, never to be changed or added to. Accept them as the absolute truth and live according to their teachings. That is the way of living a Christian life.

## Desire Righteousness

My mission as a prison minister has been to bring the Word of God to the incarcerated as a way to help them get through the unimaginable trial of losing freedom, dignity, and even hope. Having Jesus in their life and believing in Him is the way to move forward to a new existence of goodness, respectability, honesty, and decency. Regrettably, not everyone has the desire to make that choice. Some are living in their comfort zone, a society established by their peers, and have little or no interest in abandoning their present ways. My challenge is to spark their awareness and interest in a better approach to life through knowing and trying to live by the teachings of Jesus. It can be ambitious and at times problematic, but when it does take place, it sure is rewarding to witness.

*Life with Jesus*

I remember an inmate who wanted to change his ways but always had a reason why he was not able to do so. He had been in and out of prison numerous times but never took full responsibility for his actions. Although he called himself a Christian, he, as many of the inmates I visit with, knew little about Christianity. In other words, he was a Christian in name only. Regrettably, that represents an unacceptable percentage of those professing to be Christian. Being a Christian requires knowing, accepting, and believing all of Jesus's teachings. Christianity is not just a word; it is a way of life on earth, having a grand prize of eternal salvation. It is being a disciple of Jesus, and that means to accept Him as the Savior who, through His ultimate sacrifice on the cross, gave us the pathway to forgiveness of our sins and eternal salvation.

*"God so loved the world that He gave His only begotten Son, that whoever believes in Him should not perish but have everlasting life" (John 3:16).*

Accepting Jesus is believing in Him and the righteousness of His teachings. This is necessary to guide us to victory over the troublesome temptations of life. There will be times, because of the spiritual weakness of our humanity that we will sin in either thought, words, or action. Jesus realizes that and never will abandon us. It sure is comforting to know that He is always there waiting for us to return to Him. For He is our Sheppard, and we are His sheep.

*"Let us not grow weary while doing good, for in due season we shall reap if we do not lose heart"*
*(Galatians 6:9).*

---

## Who Is Jesus?

He is the only begotten Son of God the Father, the Savior of all mankind, and the second Person of the blessed Trinity. He was in the beginning, is now, and always will be.

*"In the beginning, was the Word, and the Word was with God, and the Word was God" (John 1:1).*

*"Jesus said to them, 'Most assuredly, I say to you, before Abraham was, I AM'" (John 8:58).*

*"I and My Father are one" (John 10:30).*

*"Most assuredly, I say to you, he who believes in Me has everlasting life" (John 6:47).*

*He is our Shepherd*

There are many people who believe that Jesus was just a good person, a preacher, but is not the Son of God.

Of course, we Christians know that that is false. The truth is that Jesus is the only begotten Son of God, our Savior, who came into this world as a divine being but also had a human nature. His mission was to bring truth and grace to humanity and to suffer an unimaginable death nailed to a cross for the forgiveness of our sins. He took our sins upon Himself and by doing so, out of His unconditional love for us, He opened the door to salvation.

## He Taught Us

**That salvation is a need of everyone.**

*"Not everyone who says to Me, 'Lord, Lord,' shall enter the kingdom of heaven, but he who does the will of My Father in heaven" (Matthew 7:21).*

**That God loves all of us, regardless of our life status.**

*"God so loved the world that He gave His only begotten Son, that whoever believes in Him*

*should not perish but have everlasting life" (John 3:16).*

## That forgiveness is for all people.

*"Let all bitterness, wrath, anger, clamor, and evil speaking be put away from you, with all malice. And be kind to one another, tenderhearted, forgiving one another, even as God in Christ forgave you" (Ephesians 4:31–32).*

## That faith is a way to salvation.

*"By grace you have been saved through faith, and that not of yourselves; it is the gift of God" (Ephesians 2:8).*

## The good news of the kingdom of God.

*"It came to pass, afterward, that He went through every city and village, preaching and bringing the glad tidings of the kingdom of God. And the twelve were with Him" (Luke 8:1).*

# 11

# Our Everyday Actions

Jesus also taught us of our obligation to be His disciples. Being so requires acceptance of His teachings and the commitment to inform others of that obligation through the use of our words and actions. Being His disciple does not mean that a person is expected to be a preacher of the gospel. Very few have that special calling. However, just our everyday actions and conversations will be noticed and could have a dramatic effect on others and their way of life. Jesus also educated us on how to break unhealthy habits, not give up, not be greedy, make correct choices, have patience, pray, and always practice that wonderful virtue of humility. Humility can at times be strongly overshadowed by pride and self-admiration, resulting in having an egotistical, pretentious, and judgmental point of view. That is not the way Jesus wants us to act.

Jesus, knowing that the Father had given all things
into His hands, and that He had come from God
and was going to God, rose from supper and laid aside
His garments, took a towel and girded Himself. After
that, He poured water into a basin and began to wash
the disciples' feet, and to wipe *them* with the towel
with which He was girded.

— John 13:3–5

*Jesus washes His disciples' feet*

Jesus showed us the importance of humility. He was not suggesting that we wash people's feet; He was telling us that we are all created equal and our present life position does not change that. It does not matter whether we are wealthy, just getting by, or poor. Our final judgment will be influenced by our faith and deeds, but not faith alone or deeds alone, and our status in life will not make any difference to God's judgment.

> *"As the body without the spirit is dead, so faith without works is dead also" (James 2:26).*

Do you want to be a disciple of Jesus? If so, have faith, be humble and strive for humility. By your deeds, make a difference not only in your life on earth but also in your quest for a heavenly eternity.

Go back two thousand-plus years and imagine yourself listening to Jesus's teaching in the temple. The Pharisees, among others, were listening with amazement to His words. However, the Pharisees were there for only one reason—to try to entrap Him. They were the Jewish legal experts and the dominant school of thought within the Jewish faith. They believed in God, an afterlife, and a Messiah. However, they did not accept Jesus as the Messiah. How could a carpenter's son from Jerusalem be the Messiah? Most importantly to them, Jesus was a political threat to the preservation of their way of life and their interpretation of their religious laws.

## Fear of the Outcome

Jewish coexistence with their conquerors, the Romans, was a fragile one. If the people were to accept Jesus as the Messiah, that would place Him above Nero, the Roman Emperor, who considered himself a god. Nero in turn would order the destruction of the Jewish temple and self-rule. The Pharisees could not let that outcome come to fruition and therefore were looking for an opportunity to arrest and execute Jesus, which they eventually did.

*The Roman rule*

Sometimes we are not happy with the results of particular situations. The outcome for some can result in illness, confusion, anger, and even hatred, each of which usually ends in a destructive spiritual and possible physical illness. In these times of a world pandemic, there is civil unrest and, more dire than imaginable, a visible worldwide lack of faith in the Almighty, with an outright disregard of His teachings. Many ask why God is letting this happen. Is He punishing us? The answer is an emphatic no. It is not God's fault; it is man's fault.

We are punishing ourselves by accepting a lifestyle that

has a minimum or no dependence at all on Him.

## Speak to Him

When was the last time you spoke to God, or have you ever frankly spoken to Him? The answer might be "I talk to Him when I pray." That is excellent, and I am sure that those prayers are received with immense pleasure. Are they scripted, penned words or are you talking to God as your friend? He is your creator and the best Friend you could ever have. When you pray, explain things to Him in your own words, the same way you would talk to any friend. Talk about your problems, whatever they might be, and if needed, ask for His help. You are not going to hear His actual words, but you will without question know that He has heard you and that He will guide you to a successful resolution.

We all have heard the saying that no man is an island. How true that is. The meaning of those few words emphasizes the need of others in our life. We are social beings from the time we are born till the day we depart from this earth. As youngsters, we need the protection and comfort of our parents; as teenagers and throughout life, we seek compatible friendships. All along during our life journey, we were never alone. For we always had a Friend waiting for us to accept and welcome Him into our lives—a Friend who unconditionally loves us and is just waiting to be acknowledged, a Friend who will be there for us regardless of the conditions relating to our needs. He is our personal bodyguard, patiently looking forward to our acceptance of Him as our Savior and request for His divine guidance.

*Talk to Jesus, your Friend*

# He Will Guide You

If He is my creator and loves me unconditionally, why do I need to ask for His guidance? Good question. The simple answer is that all people have been created with the magnificent gift of free will. We are all able to make decisions as we see fit, and sometimes the decisions made are not spiritually or socially acceptable. Thus, when we go against Jesus's teachings, we are pushing Him away from us. We must know Him to need Him. The only way to truly know and believe in Him is through His teachings. How can a person acknowledge and accept someone without a complete understanding of what that person stands for? If you are seeking answers about Jesus and His teachings, they will be found in the Holy Bible.

You owe it to yourself to know the truth.

*"Therefore humble yourselves under the mighty hand of God, that He may exalt you in due time, casting all your care upon Him, for He cares for you" (1 Peter 5:6–7).*

# Do You Know Him?

An inmate at the jail where I serve was attending his first Bible study class. As in many instances, the need for divine help is realized only when a traumatic event occurs. He appeared to be in his twenties. He had the presence of a very troubled person, and was facing the unknown aspects of being incarcerated. He thought that he was a Christian but knew little about Jesus or His teachings. As I have mentioned in my other books, I never ask a prisoner what he is accused of. However, in this particular case, a few weeks later, the reason for his arrest became public knowledge. He was charged with a serious felony involving a young teenage girl and, if convicted, he would be in prison for many years. Also, being an illegal immigrant, he most likely would be deported upon completion of his sentence.

Before His arrest, he was a farmworker and had been in this country, trouble free for ten years. He had plans for a bright future and someday becoming an American citizen. Now that objective was just a shattered dream never to be realized. He knew that what took place was morally wrong, and now he had no choice but to accept the legal punishment imposed. However, he did have another option, a spiritual one—the most important one he would ever make—and that was to know his Savior, Jesus Christ. Did he make that choice? I do not know, but I pray that our Bible study session, through the power of the Holy Spirit, opened his heart to the loving arms of Jesus and that he accepted Him as his personal Savior. By doing so, he would finally realize that the Lord will always be there, hear his prayers, and guide him to a new beginning. The past can never be changed, but, by his seeking forgiveness and repenting, the dark stain of evil will forever be removed from his soul.

I only saw him one time and that was because a plea bargain was accepted, and he now is serving the imposed sentence at one of the Florida State prisons. Hopefully, he will continue to pursue Jesus through the many Christian study programs offered to those incarcerated. If he does so, his life will forever be changed for his newfound best Friend will always be present to guide him through the evil temptations of life.

*"Seek first the kingdom of God and His righteousness, and all these things shall be added to you"*
*(Matthew 6:33).*

*Know Jesus, know life*

# 12

# Trails and Turmoil

Life is full of complexity, unrest, and bewilderment, and without spiritual guidance, all of this can certainly result in a lack of inner peace. It does not have to be that way for once we understand and accept that it is through the teachings, crucifixion, and resurrection of Jesus that we have been given the way to a more harmonious presence on earth. Yes, there always will be turmoil in our lives. Whatever the strife is, it can usually be managed by the calming effect of knowing that divine help is available for the asking. Let us not forget that we are human, and our humanity is subjected to the trials of life.

There are many great, inspiring stories in the Bible focusing on the trials of humanity, choosing the light of goodness or the consequences of surrendering to the darkness of evil. One such story is found in the Old Testament's book of Ruth.

## Ruth

The book of Ruth was written around 950 BC and is a story about a woman's immeasurable love, self-sacrifice, and devotion. Her name was Ruth, and all the previously mentioned accolades were directed to her relationship with her mother-in-law, Naomi. It was a time in history when the people of Moab, a pagan country, did not have moral directives to live by. Their land was a land of individual relativism where anything based on one's self-justification was acceptable. Does that relativistic way of life sound familiar? I am sure it does. It is to a great extent the way it is in today's society, especially where religious doctrine is concerned.

In the book of Ruth, the story primarily centers around Naomi, Ruth, and Boaz. It starts with Naomi, her husband, and her two sons leaving Judea during a time of famine, in search of food. They eventually settled in the foreign pagan country of Moab, where their sons married Moabite women. All was going well, and the close family looked forward to a promising future and a new beginning. That was not to be. Naomi's husband and two sons died, leaving her in the strange country with Moabite daughters-in-law, Orpah and Ruth. The loss of her husband and sons led Naomi to believe that God was punishing her for leaving Judea, the promised land, and settling in the pagan country of Moab.

Naomi decided to return to Bethlehem and to accept her fate, whatever it might be. How she was to survive was now in the hands of a loving and forgiving God. She explained to her daughters-in-law that they should stay in their homeland, return to their families, and have a new beginning. Orpah did, but not Ruth. Ruth had a sincere love for Naomi and pledged to never leave her and to take care of her for as long as she lived. She promised Naomi that she would worship the God of Israel, the one true God who loves and accepts all people. Her kindness, loyalty, faithfulness, and belief in God brought them safely back to Judea.

Ruth showed unconditional love toward Naomi by placing her well-being ahead of her own. Her unselfishness was soon rewarded by God. She found work harvesting grain. Ruth kept her promise to take care of Naomi in every conceivable way. She would rise early every day and work in the fields. When her backbreaking work was over, she and others would gather for themselves the leftover grain.

*Ruth gathered the leftover grain*

The land was owned by a wealthy man named Boaz who took a liking to Ruth. Not only was he wealthy but he was also a kind, thoughtful man of God. They soon married, and Ruth and Naomi's lives were forever changed.

The Lord works in strange ways, and the story of Ruth is an example. When all looks bleak and the gloom of helplessness begins to set in, trust in the Lord for He will never leave those who believe in Him.

> *"Trust in the Lord with all your heart,*
> *And lean not on your own understanding;*
> *In all your ways acknowledge Him,*
> *And He shall direct your paths" (Proverbs 3:5–6).*

## Seek Goodness

The choices throughout our lives are ours to make—choices some will be confronted with on a more frequent basis than others. It will be a victory or defeat outcome depending on the individual's religious strength or weakness.

If we seek goodness and moral excellence first, there will be far more victories than defeats.

Some who are reading this are thinking, *That does not concern me, for it only relates to serious, sinful decisions.* Is that so? How about gossip, slander, meddling, and spreading rumors, to name a few. They might not seem important, but they are morally wrong. Ask yourself, is that what Jesus would do? I believe the answer would immediately become apparent if the gift of wisdom is used.

One of the Bible stories that illustrates the value of having an emphasis on wisdom rather than excessive material gains is the many gifts offered by God to Solomon, king of Israel. It was in a dream that God came to him and offered whatever gifts he desired, such as fame, wealth, courage, and anything else he asked for. All he wanted was the wisdom to justly govern the people of Israel. God was so pleased with his response that in addition to wisdom, all else was also given to him. Solomon believed having wisdom was far more important than any other material gift. It was his desire to make the best choices as a ruler through wisdom, and to be available for any people seeking his advice. Can you imagine what a different world this would be if our leaders took the advice of King Solomon?

*King Solomon's wisdom was from God*

# 13

# Gratefulness

Have you ever gone into a house of worship, just sat there, and experienced the serenity of silence and knowing that God is present? It's so peaceful and comforting. If you have not, try it for it could be a life-changing experience. No longer are you surrounded by the vastness of evil that seems to be engulfing our increasingly godless society? You don't have to ask God for anything for He already knows what you need. How about just saying thank you to God? Thank you for all that you have given me. Unfortunately, thanklessness is by far more prevalent.

Luke 17:11–19 illustrates the thanklessness of nine of the ten lepers who were cured by Jesus of leprosy—a horrible, debilitating, and deadly disease because at that time in history, it was incurable. Those infected were isolated from their community and family, left to experience a slow, torturous death. That was soon to change for ten men. Jesus was on His way to Jerusalem when off in the distance, He heard their voices calling out and asking Him to have mercy on them. That He did. It was out of compassion and love that the ten were completely healed and all traces of the deadly disease were immediately removed from their deformed bodies. They were then instructed to go into the village and show the priests that they were cured by what only could be a God-given miracle. Now they could assimilate into village life once again and be with their families. What a gift!

One would think that their first move would be to find Jesus and offer thanks. That was not so. Of the ten lepers cured, only one, a Samaritan, returned to where Jesus was to give thanks for giving him his life back. Then Jesus said, "Were there not ten cleansed? But where *are* the nine? Were there not any found who returned to give glory to God except this foreigner?'

And He said to him, "Arise, go your way. Your faith has made you well'" (17–19).

*The one thankful, cured leper*

Too often, our conversations with God are about what we want and not what we have received. *Even if we do not think so*, we all have so much to thank Him for. Just consider all that He has given you. Of course, you have had many disappointments in life; we all have. Sometimes the answers to why might not be readily available, and maybe they never will be. That is when faith, trust, and belief in our Lord are necessary.

*Dwelling on the negativity of what you do not have can*

*never be constructive.* Whatever difficulties we have encountered or will experience in the future cannot possibly compare to the suffering that Jesus willingly endured for our salvation.

# 14

# Obedience

When God created Adam and Eve, He intended that all humanity would exist forever in paradise. At that time, there was no sin or death. But because our first parents disobeyed God's command, they were expelled from the garden of Eden, and thus, disobedience and the stain of original sin has been passed on to all generations. However, out of God's unconditional love for His creation, He sent His only begotten Son, Jesus, to teach us righteousness. He, through His crucifixion, became the sacrificial Lamb who granted us forgiveness of sin and gave us a pathway to eternal salvation. He is not forcing His teachings on us. It is our choice to accept or reject them. That is what free will is all about.

It was because of God's unconditional love for His creation that Jesus, our Savior, came to teach us how to cope with the difficulties of life and, most important of all, to show us through His teachings and ultimate sacrifice how to find our way home. If we use our free will as it was intended, our reward will be an eternity in paradise, where we always belonged.

Before your all-important decision is reached, be diligent and objective in seeking answers that will forever change your life. Have an open mind, seek the truth, and righteousness will prevail.

# Moses

Through Moses, God gave us the Ten Commandments, never to be added to or modified in any way. He instructed Joshua to command the Israelites to repeat them frequently lest they forget. The Ten Commandments, along with the teachings of Jesus, are a gift of love and a passport to our heavenly home. Together with the Beatitudes, they give us the glowing light of righteousness, which will always guide us through the trials of life. Some mistakenly believe that the laws of God were a way to punish His creation because of their sinful ways. No, not at all. On the contrary, they were given out of His unconditional love to save humanity from a life of self-indulgence, out-of-control unrighteousness, and moral decay.

The Ten Commandments were given to Moses by God for a reason, and that reason was to let all God-fearing men know what He expected of them. It was a list of ten laws to live by and the failure to do so often led to serious sin which, without repentance, could result in forever-lasting punishment at God's discretion. God also let it be known that the Commandments are to be accepted and followed without exception. To some that might seem pretty harsh. God, however, is never to be questioned. He is always to be loved and obeyed by those who acknowledge Him as the one and only supreme Being, our creator.

# The Ten Commandments

*Moses and the God-given Ten Commandments*

God spoke all these words, saying:

"I *am* the Lord your God,... You shall have no other gods before Me. ...

"You shall not take the name of the Lord your God in vain, ...

"Remember the Sabbath day, to keep it holy. ...

"Honor your father and your mother, ...

"You shall not murder.

"You shall not commit adultery.

"You shall not steal.

"You shall not bear false witness against your neighbor.

"You shall not covet your neighbor's house; you shall not covet your neighbor's wife, ... nor anything that *is* your neighbor's."

—Exodus 20:1–26

Jesus taught us how to live by God's laws and gave us the obligation of obeying them as a prerequisite to goodness and His ultimate gift of a glorious eternity. Sometimes owing to one's complicity, a shallowness develops regarding God's teachings. Once that becomes apparent, and the desire for change is the response. Only then will we be given the spiritual key to unlock the despair and turmoil brought on by the gloom of wrongdoing. That spiritual key is wisdom, the outstanding gift from God which comes to us through Jesus Christ. His teachings of love, forgiveness, humility, and believing open the pathway to salvation and release us from the overpowering branch of destruction.

# The Beatitudes (Blessings)

Blessed are the poor in spirit,

For theirs is the kingdom of heaven.

Blessed are those who mourn,

For they shall be comforted.

Blessed are the meek,

For they shall inherit the earth.

Blessed are those who hunger and thirst for right-

eousness,

For they shall be filled.

Blessed are the merciful,

For they shall obtain mercy.

Blessed are the pure in heart,

For they shall see God.

Blessed are the peacemakers,

For they shall be called sons of God.

Blessed are those who are persecuted for right-

eousness' sake,

For theirs is the kingdom of heaven.

Blessed are you when they revile and persecute you,

and say all kinds of evil against you falsely for My

sake. Rejoice and be exceedingly glad, for

great is your reward in heaven, for so they persecuted the prophets who were before you.

— Matthew 5:1–12

*"The wise man's eyes are in his head,*
*But the fool walks in darkness.*
*Yet I myself perceived*
*That the same event happens to them all" (Ecclesiastes 2:14).*

The "wise" prudently use the gift of wisdom as a means to righteousness whereas the "fool" disregards that gift, frequently resulting in making poor choices. If we follow the Ten Commandments and the Beatitudes, we will not walk in darkness for our choices will be the light of goodness.

Many believe that the importance of obeying the Ten Commandments is no longer a requirement for salvation as long as we believe in Jesus. That is not correct. To believe in Jesus, we must believe in what He has revealed to us, and that is His teachings, the Beatitudes, and the Ten Commandments (Exodus 20:1–

26). God did not say to Moses, "Here they are, individuals can now decide which ones they want to obey." They all were and always will be the laws of God, mandatory to live by to achieve righteousness and the way to salvation.

The importance of each commandment is referenced by Jesus throughout the New Testament. A few verses are:

> *"Blessed are those who do His commandments,*
> *that they may have the right to the tree of*
> *life, and may enter through the gates into the city"*
> *(Revelation 22:14).*

> *"Do not think that I came to destroy the Law or*
> *the Prophets. I did not come to destroy but to ful-*
> *fill" (Matthew 5:17).*

> *"If you want to enter into life, keep the command-*
> *ments" (Matthew 19:17).*

The Ten Commandments of God tell us what we must not do whereas the Beatitudes of Jesus, in almost a poetic way, motivate us to a life of righteousness through Christian ideology and behavior. The Beatitudes are the pathway to salvation and the gift of inner peace as we face the numerous trials of life.

*Obey Jesus as you walk with Him*

Some say they understand the importance of living a spiritual, ethical, and honorable life but do not accept obeying the Ten Commandments as a need for salvation. What a mistake that is. Do not try to rewrite the Bible to suit your subjective interpretation of the words of God.

He created us to be in paradise, but because of Adam

and Eve's expulsion from Eden, death became a reality. However, out of extreme love for all humanity, His only begotten Son, Jesus, came to us, conquered death, and showed us the way to a reward of eternal bliss.

Too frequently, a person might express their anger by using God's name in an expletive manner. That unacceptable vulgarity is both degrading and despicable. Never lose sight of who God is. He is our creator, a loving God who is always deserving of and demanding respect.

# 15

# Fear Free

Every once in a while, we need to take time to reflect on life in general and think of what it has given us, not what it has not given us. Everything cannot always be the way you expect it to be. If it is perfection you are looking for, you will not find it on earth for perfection can only be found in heaven. However, trying to live a life of righteousness will be a huge step forward to achieving your crown of glory and an eternity of perfection and happiness in paradise.

All human beings will go through life struggles—some very serious such as illness, death of a family member, drug and alcohol addiction, moral decay, depression, and other demons—which are little by little destroying the core of one's existence. They might feel themselves falling deeper and deeper into that forever bottomless darkness with no way out. No, it does not have to be that way for there is a way out, and that way is to seek help from God, who loves you unconditionally. It will not happen overnight, but it will happen as long as you have faith and trust in Him. Do not give up. Have strength and courage, which is a gift given to all by God.

*"God has not given us a spirit of fear, but of power and of love and of a sound mind" (2 Timothy 1:7).*

## You Can Confront the Fear

Fear because of our humanity is common for all people to experience at various times throughout their lives. It is through the control of fear that the strength of courage becomes a reality. When not controlled, fear can be so overpowering that it can paralyze one's ability to act courageously. For example, a police officer exposing himself to imminent danger, a firefighter entering a flaming building to rescue a person, a military man facing enemy fire while trying to save a fellow soldier, and it goes on and on. From each, their ability to control fear empowered the courage to achieve their courageous goals. The same holds for all levels of society: the fear of not being prepared for an exam, the fear of flying, the fear of darkness, the fear of not having the ability to provide for one's family, and the fears of those incarcerated. To defeat the anxiety of fear, the fear itself has to be confronted. The good news is you do not have to face it alone. God is always available to help you confront and eliminate whatever the fear might be. Trust and believe in him for with his guidance, the darkness of fear will be conquered.

> *"The Lord is my light and my salvation;*
> *Whom shall I fear?*
> *The Lord is the strength of my life;*
> *Of whom shall I be afraid"* (Psalm 27:1).

Our life begins with having a complete physical dependence on others and usually ends in the same manner. But that ending is just the beginning of the next step, which is an eternity where the trials of life no longer exist and are replaced by perfect happiness.

*We need not fear when we walk with Jesus*

Imagine never again being separated from our loved ones, freedom from all earthly ailments and frustrations, and, most important of all, being with God, the architect of all that ever was and ever will be. That sure is something worthwhile to look forward to. It is a promise made to us by the Almighty, and He does not break His promises. "Most assuredly, I say to you, he who hears My word and believes in Him who sent Me has everlasting life, and shall not come into judgment, but has passed from death into life" (John 5:24).

# 16

# What Is Faith?

Another of the many promises of life after death, salvation, and forgiveness of sin was made by Jesus while He was dying on the cross. On each side of Him were condemned criminals who were guilty of their crimes and were also suffering the excruciating agony of crucifixion. The thief on His left was an unbeliever who denounced and berated Jesus. He wanted proof before believing that Jesus was "the Christ." The thief on Jesus's right said to him, "Do you not even fear God? Jesus is an innocent man." He then asked Jesus to remember him when He was in heaven. Jesus's reply was, "Assuredly, I say to you, today you will be with Me in Paradise" (Luke 23:43).

There are numerous definitions of the noun "eternity,"

one of which is: "a state to which time has no application; timelessness." Another is "endless life after death." I guess it can be said with the highest degree of confidence that eternity is a state of foreverness. Where we spent it is another matter.

## Do You Believe?

It is clearly stated in the Bible that forever will be either heaven or hell. We now have the choice to believe or not to believe. If we do believe, and I certainly hope so, the question of where our eternity will be spent becomes a moot one.

*"If we confess our sins, He is faithful and just to forgive us our sins and to cleanse us from all unrighteousness" (1 John 1:9).*

If the choice is to believe, then the next question is if we believe without question. In my book *Navigating through the Storms of a Christian Life*, I try to explain

116

the difference between belief and total belief as fol-
lows:

In the year 1859, there lived the greatest tightrope
walker in the world, a Frenchman named Charles Blon-
din. He planned to be the first man to cross Niagara
Falls walking on a cable. The distance of the crossing
was 1,100 feet, and the cable was three inches in diam-
eter. The height above the rocks and water was 160
feet. Thousands of people from all over the world came
to witness this first-ever daredevil feat. Charles Blon-
din was not using any safety equipment, so if he mis-
stepped, it certainly would result in his death. That did
not happen, and he was successful in making the crossing. The crowds were cheering him as they saw history
being made. He then asked if they believed he could
cross back to the other side pushing a wheelbarrow.
The spectators shouted, "Yes, you are the greatest. We
know you can do it" And he did. Once again, there was
a joyous eruption of praise from all the spectators. He
then shouted, "Do you think I can cross to the other side
with a person in the wheelbarrow?" Once again, the
spontaneous response was yes. Charles then shouted

back, "Who will volunteer to sit in the wheelbarrow?" He had no takers.

They believed in his greatness but did not believe beyond question. If they had sincerely believed in him, he would have had many volunteers. Is it time to ask yourself, do you believe in Jesus without question?

If not, why is that? Is there Scripture that is questioned, or is it that you think the Bible as a whole lacks credibility? As stated previously the credibility of both the Old and New Testaments has been verified by the finding and reconstruction of the Dead Sea Scrolls. Before denying, use your God-given gift of wisdom for a better understanding of what is being denied. Read the Bible and then make your choice. That sacred Book is God's blueprint for the salvation of all. Nowhere in that masterpiece does God say you have the option of accepting some of His teachings but rejecting others. There are no options. To be Christians, we must believe and accept all His teachings.

*"Whoever shall keep the whole law, and yet stumble in one point, he is guilty of all" (James 2:10).*

The Ten Commandments and the teachings of Jesus Christ were given to all out of unconditional love. They are not to punish us. On the contrary, they are to reward us with an eternal gift of living where we always were meant to be, namely in paradise.

## Understanding the Bible

It can at times require uninterrupted concentration to understand a scripture's sacred meaning. Ask the Holy Spirit to give you the wisdom to recognize the intended significance, and try to stay focused on the knowledge that the words you are reading come from Almighty God.

*"The Revelation of Jesus Christ, which God gave Him to show His servants—things which must shortly take place. And He sent and signified it by His angel to His servant John" (Revelation 1:1).*

*An angel appeared to John*

I have been blessed to be a prison minister for many years. Before the onset of the pandemic, we would have Bible study sessions every week. Before each meeting, I would ask the Holy Spirit to grant me the capability to understand the intended meaning of the scripture passages to be discussed. Too often a person might just read Scripture without having a clear understanding of the writer's intent. I always say, read a sentence, dwell on it for a while, then continue. In one of my Bible study sessions, we read and discussed the meaning of Jesus's words in Matthew 17:20: "Assuredly, I say to you, if you have faith as a mustard seed, you will say to this mountain, 'Move from here to there,' and it will move; and nothing will be impossible for you." There were a few different interpretations of that passage from those in attendance, but one, in particular, stood out. The inmate took the passage word for word, believing if his faith were strong enough, he would have the power to move the location of a mountain. Why did he believe that? Because that is what Jesus said. Yes, He did say that. However, what the inmate did not realize was that it was Jesus's way of making a point illustrated by a story. Jesus was telling us of the immense power of even a small amount of faith and what can be accomplished through it.

## The Power of Faith

We are not perfect, and by inheriting original sin, we have imperfections in our lives that can and do become obstacles to righteousness. However, the power of faith is so immense that even a small amount is sufficient to move those demons out of our life. I am sure

121

that some will disagree and say I do not believe that that reading applies to me. I believe it does pertain to all human beings, for everyone is a sinner.

Jesus told His apostles the parables depended on His audience. For His apostles, Jesus used short parables to inspire their reasoning and teach a moral or spiritual lesson. When we read a parable, we should always ask ourselves what Jesus wants to teach us through it.

# A Solid Foundation

Life is a journey through time. Our journey is not always going to be a smooth one. There will be many bumps along the way that will test the strength of our faith and highlight the need for a solid foundation of truth to believe in. That foundation is Jesus. Without him in our lives, weakness will overpower the need for strength when confronted with the inevitable storms of life.

"Whoever hears these sayings of Mine, and does them, I will liken him to a wise man who built his house on the rock: and the rain descended, the floods came, and the winds blew and beat on that house; and it did not fall, for it was founded on the rock.

"But everyone who hears these sayings of Mine, and does not do them, will be like a foolish man who built his house on the sand: and the rain descended, the floods came, and the winds blew and beat on that house; and it fell. And great was its fall."

—Matthew 7:24–27

Jesus pointed out the necessity for a solid foundation of faith to defeat the enticement of unrighteousness. He likened it to two men: one whose faith was not substantial and could not stand up to the evils of temptation, the other whose strong foundation of faith *could* withstand the storms of wrongdoing. Jesus wants us not only to hear His words but to live according to them. Then and only then will we be prepared for what is destined for all people—judgment.

*Just like the prodigal son's father, the Father is always happy to welcome you home*

# 17

# What Influences Us?

Sometimes we will be the victor and other times we will lose the battle and succumb to the darkness of unrighteousness. Some will say, "That is not me. I am not a sinner." Yes, you are; we all are. To make that statement, a person should be sure of what constitutes a sin. The simple answer is willful disobedience of the Ten Commandments and the teachings of Jesus. An example is, the seventh commandment, "Thou shall not bear false witness against thy neighbor." Another is jealousy, the tenth commandment "Thou shall not covet thy neighbor's goods."

What are we looking for out of life? The answer for many will probably be success, health, and happiness, all of which are attributed to our temporary state of existence.

## A Long-Term Perspective

What our goals of achievement should be based on is our permanent existence of eternal life, a life in paradise that is available to all. Unfortunately, in this world of chaos, moral decline, and uncertainty, there prevails for many an existence of perpetuating self-interest. Eternity is not the focal point. Many people believe that financial achievement will satisfy most requirements of being successful and will bring happiness. What a falsehood that is. I know because I experienced it.

The accomplishment of financial success usually brings only short-term happiness because our human nature tends not to be satisfied with what we have and is always seeking more. The desire for more can always be justified through what will eventually turn out to be an unrealistic subjective wish. Saint Paul said that money in itself is not evil. It is the love of money that is evil. How true that is. When money becomes the primary comfort factor, watch out for you are now heading to an imbalance between spiritual and material values.. God gave each of us the ability to achieve that which is good as long as:

- what we seek to gain is not based only on material achievement or greed, and
- it does not result in our spiritual values being compromised or becoming nonexistent.

*Always seek Jesus first*

As youngsters, our morality is being molded through

127

the actions and teachings of our parents as well as other outside influences. We depend on our parents. We believe totally in them for in our eyes, they cannot do any wrong. Obviously, because of their human nature, that is not always correct. However, it is, for the most part, the influence from parents that is needed to establish, nurture, and mold the process of growth, morally and spiritually. As we get older, peer pressure can become a serious barrier from a behavioral point of view. There will be times when undesirable influences result in values being compromised, resulting in life-changing behavior.

## Who Do You Associate With?

Association is one of the most important choices a person can make especially during his or her young, impressionable life. Sometimes the association is based on an individual's makeup of being a leader or a follower. If a leader, affiliation usually is with those of similar background, interest, and goals. They are ambitious and want to achieve their fullest potential in whatever field is selected.

Life is an encompassing experience, one of love, hate, sickness, happiness, sadness, fear, courage, and all the other emotions that makes us human. Our humanity can be considered a miraculous and extraordinary gift; however, through the misuse of free will, humanity can become a spiritual, overpowering, dark cloud of regret. When God created our world, it was never intended for mankind to experience the evil which exists today, as well as death. All that has come to be because of the misuse of free will by our first parents and their disregard of God's command. They used their free will to allow themselves to be tempted by the evil serpent, resulting in willful disobedience and unrighteous choices.

# 18

# This Temporary Life

It is through God's love and His overwhelming generosity that creation came to be. Our being is one of humanity, and that is a temporary gift that should be treasured and enjoyed through living a life of goodness. It is temporary because we do not have complete control over our longevity. Once it is over, then comes the permanent gift of eternity. One is temporary and the other permanent. Which is the one we should be most concerned about? It is the permanent one, eternity. That does not mean that our limited time on earth is not meaningful. Yes, it is. It is not only meaningful but is fundamental as to where the everafter will be spent. The choice is ours to make.

# Atheists Have No Proof

Regrettably, the goal of salvation does not have any meaning to disbelievers. Many of those individuals only see existence as being life on earth and then a vast void of nothingness. How depressing that must be. The atheists do not believe in the existence of God and the agnostics must have proof before believing. Life experiences alone should be able to convince most people of God's existence and influence in our lives. I would suggest that disbelievers take the time to thoroughly consider what brought them to that frightful conclusion. *Can they prove that God does not exist?* No, they cannot.

Some conclude that creation just happened to take place due to a series of unproven events (the Big Bang) billions of years ago, resulting in the formation of our universe and eventually the evolution of humanity? *If that is their belief, then they are correct that life after death does not exist.* What a horrible thought. We believers accept the history of creation as stated in the book of

131

Genesis—the Word of God and therefore indisputable.

## Material Possessions vs Spiritual Possessions

> Do not lay up for yourselves treasures on earth, where moth and rust destroy and where thieves break in and steal; but lay up for yourselves treasures in heaven, where neither moth nor rust destroys and where thieves do not break in and steal. For where your treasure is, there your heart will be also.
>
> — Matthew 6:19–21

A person's treasures on earth are material possessions, such as financial assets that provide for the pleasures of life. These are good as long as they are not abused by overindulgence and greed. If that does take place there will be an imbalance between our spiritual and material accomplishments. That can result in failing to seek what is truly important, namely a life seeking righteousness—our pathway to salvation.

One of the pitfalls of pursuing excessive material possessions is not knowing when enough is enough. We all have possessions, some of us more so than others. But as the Scriptures tell us, "One's life does not consist in the abundance of the things he possesses" (Luke 12:15). A successful life is not living a materialistic one but living a righteous one.

*Jesus always thanked God for his daily food*

The basic needs are food, clothing, and shelter. To many in this world achieving just those primary essentials is being able to say that my life has been a successful one. If you are fortunate enough to have the capability of accruing more than the basics of life, then do so, but do so in a manner of righteousness and not greed.

---

# What Is Success?

We all have our opinion of success and hopefully realize that success is subjective and should always be measured on an individual basis. So, it is important to realize and accept our limitations and through that process, determine what being successful means to you. Sometimes it is difficult to take that first step, but remember you are never alone. Guidance from God is always available for the asking. "Seek first the kingdom of God and His righteousness, and all these things shall be added to you. Therefore do not worry about tomorrow, for tomorrow will worry about its own things" (Matthew 6:33). Stay focused and establish a realistic goal, but most important of all, accept and follow the laws of God, which will ensure that your life is one of goodness. And that is the epitome of success.

*"I will say to my soul, 'Soul, you have many goods*

*laid up for many years; take your ease; eat,*
*drink, and be merry"' (Luke 12:19).*

---

# Selfishness

An example of selfishness and greed can be found in Luke 12:16–21—a story of a rich man whose barn was full of harvested grain. Yet, there still was more left in the field. What was he to do with the remaining yield? Rather than be satisfied with the abundance he already had stored and give the rest to the needy, he decided to remove all that was stored, destroy the existing barn, and build a new one large enough for storage of the entire crop. Now, this selfish landowner would have an overabundance lasting for many years. His focus was that of an egotistic person, thinking of only himself. He desired to live it up; eat, drink, and be merry; and enjoy the pleasures of life without the concern for what the future might hold. He didn't realize that that day was going to be his last one on earth. Was he prepared to meet the Almighty and learn of his eternal judgment? Are you? Now is the time to make things right with God. Do not put it off till tomorrow, for maybe there will not be a tomorrow.

## The Comfort of Knowing Jesus

Being a prison minister for these many years has shown me how faith, trust, and belief in Jesus Christ can gradually change one's life. Most of the people I meet with have very little knowledge of Jesus and His teachings. Yet if asked if they believe in Him, the answer without any hesitation will usually be yes. But the why part is quite vague. Therefore it is our job to explain through the Scriptures the importance of knowing who Jesus is, and not only teach about accepting His teachings but about living a life of righteousness by obeying them.

Jesus is and should be accepted through faith and trust as being our Savior, the only begotten Son of God who came to us having both a divine and human nature. Jesus gave His life for the forgiveness of our sins, and through His teachings opened the celestial gates to our heavenly salvation. He taught us to love one another, forgive, be humble, be kind, have faith, trust in Him, believe, and not be quick to judge. Hopefully, our classes not only answer their questions but can lead to an ongoing dialogue resulting in the reassuring comfort of a newfound closeness to our Lord.

*Knowing Jesus is life-changing*

*"Trust in the Lord with all your heart,*
*And lean not on your own understanding;*
*In all your ways acknowledge Him,*
*And He shall direct your paths" (Proverbs 3:5–6).*

Unfortunately, some show little interest and are primarily looking at Bible study as a means of having a few more hours out of their jail cells. We hope that through divine intervention, their interest can eventually be stimulated and lead to a desire to know about and understand the life of the greatest person who ever existed, namely, Jesus Christ. Sometimes it takes just one word to spark that interest. If it does happen, it could be the beginning of a life-changing experience where the person's emotions and actions are no longer controlled by giving in to temptations and a life of darkness. Instead, they are guided by hope and belief in having a better earthly existence with a promise of an eternal reward in paradise.

# 19

# Forgive Them

As we go through life, the importance of believing in forgiveness seems to take a greater priority. Why is that? One reason is that throughout our life, we have heard about the necessity of forgiving and its relationship to salvation. Being Christians, we certainly are aware of Jesus's words related to forgiveness. "Forgive, and you will be forgiven" Luke 6:36). The way you forgive is the way you will be forgiven. Without question, His message is telling us what He expects us to do. Knowing you will not be forgiven unless you forgive needs to be accepted and always embraced. Forgiveness is essential for one seeking salvation, and the lack of forgiveness could certainly have dire consequences not only spiritually but also physically and mentally. You have heard people say they could never forgive a person for what they said. Yes, you can forgive. Just think of Jesus dying a horrible death on a cross crying out to His Father, "Father, forgive them, for they do not know what they do" (Luke 23:34). Do you still think you cannot forgive? How about the repentant criminal who was next to Jesus? He asked for forgiveness and Jesus's response was "Today you will be with Me in Paradise" (v. 43). I know it is not easy to do, but once that forgiveness comes from the heart, you will experience an inner peace you never thought possible.

## The Poison of Unforgiveness

I have seen what the lack of forgiveness can do to an incarcerated person. It is like cancer eating away at their inner being. Their days are filled with anger and hate usually resulting in unacceptable behavior such as fighting and other disruptive actions, all of which usually have an outcome of dire disciplinary consequences.

It was during one of my discussions on forgiveness that

an inmate interrupted and said, "I will never forgive my wife." He then went on to say that she had recently made her last visit to the jail and told him that she was now living with his best friend and wanted a divorce. That was quite a traumatic moment for him. There was nothing he could do. He was in jail awaiting trial and did not have any idea when that would take place; furthermore, if convicted, how long or where he would be incarcerated. He was now experiencing a grim feeling of helplessness. Emotionally, he was being destroyed and saw no end to his anger, hatred, and desire for revenge, which grew stronger as each day passed. The result was frequent disciplinary action as well as isolation, which in turn only inflamed his emotional collapse.

Eventually, he realized that there was little, if anything, he alone could do that might change what was taking place. But he soon realized that he needed help for his mental and physical well-being, which was rapidly declining. That help would come through Jesus, who always is available with only one condition—to ask and believe in Him as our Savior. And so, he did. Would it change the inevitable outcome? No, it most likely would not. But through the grace of God, he would find hope and a new beginning that would forever change his life.

*Unchecked anger can lead to tragic consequences*

Considerable time is spent with the inmates discussing the need for forgiveness and the numerous benefits to receive by doing so. It might not happen overnight, but it will happen. Gradually, the elimination of the spiritual and physical crippling effects of hatred, anger, and the need for revenge brings a new beginning filled with inner peace and the comforting realization that we are doing what Jesus said we must do. During tough times, think of Jesus dying on the cross and asking His Father to forgive those who were killing Him. "Father, forgive them, for they do not know what they do" (Luke 23:34).

Not only is forgiveness necessary for salvation; it is a major contributor to achieving a more meaningful and peaceful existence during our temporary stay on earth. Isn't that what we want? I believe it is. Let us reach out to those who we have not yet forgiven and express to them our forgiveness for whatever their action was. By doing so, we are taking the first step in receiving the glorious gift of a heavenly eternity.

## Miracles Happen

A while back, I ran across a very inspiring story of faith, courage, and belief that I would like to share with you. This is a story that takes place in 1944 during World War II. At that time, the United States was in the process of invading the Japanese-held Marianna Islands. A lot of preparation takes place before an invasion, with intelligence being on top of the list. Unfortunately, the intelligence is not always accurate, resulting in devastating consequences, namely excessive casualties.

In this particular case, the result was just that. The intelligence information was mistaken about the number of enemy troops, which resulted in extremely high losses. In one platoon of approximately forty men, only one Marine got through the initial battle and now, without immediate help, his survival was unlikely.

He noticed a series of caves and decided if he could reach them, there was a slim chance he might survive. He did make it to a cave, but once there, it became apparent that because of its depth and openness, it soon would be all over. Physically, he prepared for his ultimate moments, knowing that he would adhere to his Marine Corps training of never surrendering. Most importantly, he was a true believer in God and knew his only chance of survival would be through divine intervention. So, he prayed, "Lord if it is your will, save me. If it is not, I accept my fate, for my love, faith, and trust in you will never falter."

He then heard the explosions of hand grenades that the enemy was throwing into each cave entrance. He was prepared for the finality to come. Then the miracle happened.

*Miracles still happen*

Unbeknown to him, the cave was also inhabited by numerous spiders who were spinning strands of web across the cave entrance, thus giving the appearance of it being unoccupied. They did not finish, but the enemy did see the spider webs and, believing the cave to be empty, went right by the entrance. The Marine survived to tell this miraculous story of never giving up and, most important of all, of God's undeniable love.

Did you ever feel that you were in a particular situation that was resulting in spiritual defeat? It could be the loss of a loved one, a job, a friendship, a financial disaster, or sickness. For many, the first thought is, *Why is God letting this happen to me?* God is not the cause. In many cases, it is the happenings of humanity. Do not give up and, most of all through prayer, seek God's divine help. He might not eliminate the problem, but if you have faith in Him, He will guide you through whatever the difficulty might be.

## Never Alone

Regardless of how serious a problem might be, we are never alone for Jesus will always be by our side, waiting for us to seek His help.

*"Have I not commanded you? Be strong and of good courage; do not be afraid, nor be dismayed, for the Lord your God is with you wherever you go" (Joshua 1:9).*

We are never alone. It might not appear that way when life is on a downward spiral, and you might seem to be heading at warp speed for an emotional collision with the unknown. Do not give up for you are not alone. When all seems lost and hope is fading into the emptiness of an eternal abyss, grab hold and do not surrender to its grasp. Always have hope, faith, and trust in the only person who always will be there for you, namely your creator and friend, Almighty God.

My Lord God, I have no idea where I am going. I do not see the road ahead of me. I cannot know for certain where it will end. Nor do I really know myself, and the fact that I think that I am following your will does not mean that I am actually doing so. But I believe that the desire to please you does in fact please you. And I hope I have that desire in all that I am doing. I hope that I never will do anything apart from that desire. And I know that if I do this you will lead me by the right road, though I may know nothing about it. Therefore, will I trust you always though I may seem to be lost and in the shadow of death. I will not fear, for you are ever with me, and you will never leave me to face my perils alone.

— Thomas Merton, *Thoughts in Solitude*

*You are never alone when you know Jesus*

## Your Wake-Up Call

How often have you heard or uttered the expression that time seems to be flying by? For most people, that appears to be the way it is. Maybe, being aware can be considered God's wake-up call reminding us to be prepared for that unbeknown hour, day, or year when it will be time to face eternity. Nothing from our earthly residence will be going with us for everything we will ever need has been in heavenly storage waiting to be claimed. The key to that celestial vault is a common one available for all mankind. It is a radiant key labeled righteousness that will be used for opening the gates into paradise and claiming our crown of glory. Unfortunately, many will not have that special key of righteousness and will be denied entrance. It does not have to be that way, and it would not be so if only we were prepared. Denial of entry into paradise is not because we are sinners, it will be because we have failed to repent and to ask our Lord for forgiveness. "Strive to enter through the narrow gate, for many, I say to you, will seek to enter and will not be able" (Luke 13:24).

# 20

---

# Conclusion

Now is the time to look in the mirror of life. *Am I pleased with what I see?* What you are looking at is the present and not the past, for when you finally accepted Jesus into your life, the past inequities were erased from your soul "never to be remembered."

> If a wicked man turns from all his sins which he has committed, keeps all My statutes, and does what is lawful and right, he shall surely live; he shall not die. None of the transgressions which he has committed shall be remembered against him; because of the righteousness which he has done, he shall live.
>
> — Ezekiel 18:21–22

**In conclusion, do not surrender to the ever-present evils of humanity, but defeat those destructive storms**

by believing in Jesus Christ and living a life of right-eousness. For righteousness on earth is the golden ticket to a triumphant eternity in heaven.

*Your welcome home*

# HAVE A GLORIOUS TRIP HOME, AND KEEP THE HEAVENLY BEACON OF LIGHT SHINING TO SHOW US THE WAY.

# About the Author

Richard DeGiacomo served as a United States Marine and is a veteran of the Korean War. After his service, he attended Boston College, where he graduated with a bachelor's degree in economics. He has had an extensive business career, and for the last fifteen years, he has been serving as a prison minister.

Richard has been married for sixty-four years to his wife, Elaine; and he has three children, six grandchildren, and four great-grandchildren.

## Contact Richard

**Email:** achristianlife3@gmail.com

**Website:** www.richarddegiacomo.com

**Books:** Available in all online bookstores such as Amazon, Barnes & Noble, etc., and on Richard's website.

# Other Books by Richard

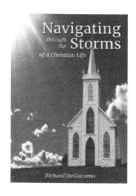

*Navigating through the Storms of a Christian Life* takes us on a journey through time and answers many of the questions we might have about our relationship with Jesus. It helps us understand who He is, why He came, what He did, and why He sacrificed Himself for the forgiveness of our sins.

*Navigating through the Storms* also explains the true meaning of Christianity and how its influence will help us get through the difficulties of this life and earn our reward of eternal salvation. Discover these truths for yourself and to learn how to walk in the ways of Jesus.

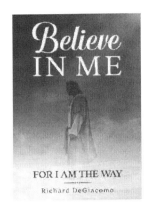

## A READER'S FAVORITE 5-STAR READ!

There is a better way to live. There is a right path to walk. *Believe in Me: For I Am the Way* is a book dedicated to those who are seeking internal peace and peace in our world. In it, Richard DeGiacomo clearly spells out how a relationship with Jesus can influence and challenge us to pursue His way to a more rewarding life on earth and a pathway to eternal salvation.

Living a well-balanced life Jesus is the only foundation we can stand on in faith, for it is through righteousness that truth becomes a reality and gives us the spiritual strength to face the trials of humanity. Read on to discover these truths for yourself and to learn how to walk in the ways of Jesus.

Made in the USA
Columbia, SC
24 February 2023